The 30 Day Life after Divorce Prayer Challenge for Women

Charis Rooks

ROYSTON
Publishing

BK Royston Publishing
P. O. Box 4321
Jeffersonville, IN 47131
502-802-5385
http://bkroystonpublishing.com
bkroystonpublishing@gmail.com

Cover Design: Bill Lacy Graphics
Layout: BK Royston Publishing LLC

ISBN-13: 9780985943998
ISBN-10: 0-9859439-9-8

Printed in the United States of America

Thank you

To my Heavenly Father I thank you father for allowing my recovery from two divorces and for turning my past hurt into my purpose and healing. Father I want to thank you again for your son, my personal Lord and Savior Jesus Christ.

In Loving Memory of Calvin and Loretta Wilson

Introduction

Prayer was one of my biggest challenges when I encountered my divorce. In my most painful moments I was so hurt and angry I could not see the benefit of prayer. Honestly the last thing I wanted to do was pray to GOD. I personally felt that God allowed this to happen to me and GOD must really not love me or like me much at all. I suffered from two divorces and God knew how hard the first one was for me but I felt God allowed it to happen again. I remember those days where I would ask God why are you so angry with me? Why would you be this awesome good God for everyone else but me? I know I have sinned but there are those out there who have done worse than me and they do not suffer like this. So after a few months of refusing to pray a friend suggested that I started to try it. So I did it not out of desperation but more to prove the theory to my friend that prayer didn't work and it wouldn't change a thing. Prayer didn't fit into my realist mentality but I had to be able to argue that it didn't work for me to win others to my way of thinking. I needed them to see through my eyes and not their clouded ideal of what prayer could do. However, once I did start to pray my life changed tremendously in every area, to the point where I now refuse to go through my day not speaking to God through prayer. If you know me you know that I'm a polar extremist either I do it 100% or I don't do it at all what can I say.

While travelling on my journey of recovery I came across many women while facilitating divorce care groups who have the same look I did back in the beginning when I would ask how is your prayer life? So I wanted to create something for women like me in mind to help in initiating their prayer life after divorce. I wanted something to reach women no matter what stage of life after divorce that they are in. So if you are a believer, non-believer, or you have no idea what in the heck is going on with you right now this book is for you.

This 30 day challenge is created so that at any point in time you can take 30 days and commit to praying. Each day has a mini story, scripture and prayer challenge. I would like to suggest that you start your prayer challenge reading with a thank you prayer each day. Your beginning prayer is a thank you to God for your life. I know I just made some of you take a double take at the last sentence so let me explain why I put this in the book for you. My reason for adding a thank you is because you are still here and you have a purpose. You may not know your purpose at this moment and that is okay. It may seem so far away from your current reality, however you must have trust and have faith in God and you will see that thanking God will grow that sense of trust that you may currently lack. Also this conditions you to start praying in a thankful mindset to God. Many times we take all our problems to God which is absolutely ok but let's take everything to God in prayer the good times, in between, and the bad. The 30 day life after divorce prayer challenge will condition you to begin praying a prayer of thankfulness for all areas of your life.

Secondly, keep in mind to please do not let the technicality of prayer keep you from this challenge like it did for me when I first started praying. God knows I was trying so hard to pray like everyone one else that sounded good and I missed the authenticity and many times the purpose of my prayer. The uniqueness in this prayer challenge is the fact that each individual will have a prayer and it will be different. There is no uniform or systematic requirement for you to pray with this challenge so do not get hung up on that. When you are hurt and broken the enemy will try to break your communication from God in every way possible. Yes one of those techniques the enemy uses is technicality. If you can be distracted then the frustration can set in and then you lose the desire to pray completely. For myself I had to also fight past this so it's okay if you get frustrated, move past it and talk to God. I began my journey of prayer just talking to God as if we were sitting together on a park bench. I cried, yelled, screamed, smiled, and even had a blank stare. However no matter what I prayed. Over the years I'm glad this was the foundation of my relationship with God because now I feel comfortable praying to God. My goal is to encourage you starting today to do the same. This is your personal relationship with God and no one else so your prayer should be yours and only yours.

After you have read each day please see the prayer challenge on the following page. I suggest you take the challenge one day at a time. This will allow you to just focus on one area that day instead of feeling overwhelmed with several challenges in one day. Don't forget the enemy will try to creep in and make you feel overwhelmed at times even when you are doing something that is for yourself. Please feel free to repeat days and even to restart when your 30 days have been completed. The beauty in this is our prayers will change with the seasons of our lives, so I encourage you to continue to pray daily. Think of this as your course syllabus for class. I'm outlining the course objective but you must apply it yourself.

To the woman that holds this book in her hand

My Prayer is that you are able to see through this challenge that God put you here for a reason, he created you, he molded you, and he has and always will love you, do not ever forget that. Though it may seem that you are getting an unfair end of the stick, or you're overwhelmed with brokenness this too shall pass. Lean on God and know that God will never leave you nor forsake you. Let God see you through this. – Charis

"Trust in the LORD with all your heart, and lean not on your own understanding; in all your ways acknowledge Him, and He shall direct your paths."
Proverbs 3:5-6

Day 1

Today begin with your thank you prayer for being alive and having a life purpose that is dedicated to God's use.

"And we know that in all things God works for the good of those who love him, who have been called according to his purpose" (Romans 8:28).

For some there are moments that may occur in your life where you say to yourself "I'm here after divorce now what"? There are so many suggestions and ideas from family and friends it can make you feel over whelmed. When I think of these suggestions I think of clothing in a clothing store. In today's society there are several clothing options, however I have yet to see a woman go into clothing store and buy items for herself that do not fit. That's just not practical, for example, the average woman would not buy herself a pair of pants out of the newborn section. No, instead she will shop for her own particular style and size that is specific to her needs and liking. So why do we take every piece of advice after divorce and try to apply it to our lives? Some may argue and may say I did it out of desperation. I would then ask you out of desperation would you run to the newborn section of a clothing store to buy business attire for an interview? Sounds unrealistic and borderline crazy, however, this is exactly what you are doing in your life by trying every suggestion. Yes we have loved ones and families who have our best interest in mind however, their advice is what they want to see for us at times. This isn't a bad thing. In fact, in some cases they love us enough to want to help. However, what is dangerous is the fact that their advice is what THEY want to see for our lives and this may not be what GOD wants for our lives. The best way to handle multiple suggestions from those who love you would be to select and pray regarding the suggestion that applies to your particular need at that point in time. In other words, suggestions of dating the day after your divorce would not be as much of a wise priority suggestion as would a family member discussing with you ways to save your money and invest as a single woman. Remember to thank your family and friends for their love and concern for you and then pray over the suggestions. If your spirit says move on it then you do just that. You move to the next phase which is applying that suggestion to your particular situation. If you are not feeling well about a suggestion and you find yourself debating or polling others then I bet it's safe to say that this is not a suggestion that should take priority right now in your situation. I'm not saying you will never need it, I'm saying just for now it should be revisited when you feel more comfortable with the suggestion and application of it in your life.

Prayer Challenge

Ask God to place people along your path that will trigger a light bulb when they share the message and suggestions God wants you to hear personally.

Proverbs 20:18 "Plans succeed through good counsel; don't go to war without wise advice."

_____

_____

_____

_____

_____

_____

_____

_____

_____

_____

_____

_____

_____

_____

_____

_____

_____

_____

_____

_____

_____

Day 2

Today begin with your thank you prayer for being alive and having a life purpose that is dedicated to God's use.

"And we know that in all things God works for the good of those who love him, who have been called according to his purpose" (Romans 8:28).

The first 3 days without my ex-husband in our home was terrifying for me. I could not sleep because I was constantly checking windows, doors, kids, and then I would start the rotation all over again until daylight. After those three days passed by I noticed I would lie down but I couldn't really sleep the way my body wanted me to sleep. I was mentally and physically exhausted and on top of that I was sleep deprived. I remember my fear was there were only three of us and no male protector in our home anymore, in those moments I felt overwhelmingly vulnerable. It's moments like these that scripture tells us, specifically, that we can go to bed without fear. I have come to notice that with divorce we tend believe fear more so than scripture, I can definitely testify to this. For you it may not be a fear of being alone however, fear is fear regardless of the reason or situation. Maybe your fear came in the form of a financial burden after the divorce.

How will the mortgage get paid or how will I put food on the table? Did your nights become sleepless? Or maybe how will I be able to do everything that we planned for our future now on my own? Or maybe you are saying to yourself that you were barely keeping to a schedule with both of you in the household, so how in the world can you maintain structure alone? There are several reasons and fear of the unknown seems to be the common denominator. I remember when I finally began to say to myself "God you did not give me the spirit of fear." I received an overwhelming sense of peace. I will be honest it wasn't a onetime thing. I said it daily and sure enough I began to sleep more and more peacefully as time went on. I began to check the doors less and less until I would check the doors one time and the kids once and I was out like a light bulb. Scripture not only tells us that God gave us a sound mind but we can go to bed without fear and sleep soundly.

Prayer Challenge

Ask God to give you peace in any area you need.

Proverbs 3:24 "you can go to bed without fear; you will lie down and sleep soundly."

_____

_____

_____

_____

_____

_____

_____

_____

_____

_____

_____

_____

_____

_____

_____

_____

_____

_____

_____

Day 3

Today begin with your thank you prayer for being alive and having a life purpose that is dedicated to God's use.

"And we know that in all things God works for the good of those who love him, who have been called according to his purpose" (Romans 8:28).

There will be times where you will want more than what you have. I would get angry with God for the struggles that I experienced. I was also angry that I didn't have much money and the fact that I didn't have it was what I feared the most. The bible says that you cannot worship money and God so you will have to ultimately decide. I found that when I gave my life completely to Christ I didn't have the same needs. I saw life through a different pair of lenses. I gave my burdens to God and I was thankful for life and what new adventure God would show me. Worrying about money started to decrease and focusing on what God had in store for me started to increase.

Prayer Challenge

Pray for satisfaction with what you have and not to focus on what you do not have.

Proverb 15:16 "Better to have little, with fear for the LORD, than to have great treasure and inner turmoil."

_____

_____

_____

_____

_____

_____

_____

_____

_____

_____

_____

_____

_____

_____

_____

_____

_____

_____

_____

_____

_____

_____

_____

_____

_____

_____

_____

_____

_____

_____

_____

_____

_____

_____

_____

_____

_____

_____

_____

_____

_____

_____

_____

_____

_____

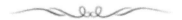

Day 4

Today begin with your thank you prayer for being alive and having a life purpose that is dedicated to God's use.

"And we know that in all things God works for the good of those who love him, who have been called according to his purpose" (Romans 8:28).

One of the hardest things to do after any divorce is to accept discipline. I remember sitting in front of a financial advisor a year after my second divorce. She was going over some things with me and I became very argumentative. I had excuses for all my financial mistakes and it was all due to the divorce. I was so negative that she looked me in the eye and said I cannot teach you if you're not willing to learn. I looked at her really funny and followed my look with "what did you just say to me"? She repeated herself and I walked out. I hated that she was correcting me and teaching me how to be more disciplined with my financial matters. Isn't that crazy how I acted when I came to her to help me be more disciplined in the areas of financial matters, because she was the expert? Does that sound familiar to any of you? We all have encountered this sometime in our lives. But it's funny how God will bring you full circle regardless of how you feel. A year later I was sitting in front of her again because I was ready now. I had to humble myself and ask her to please show me the correct way to make financial investments and decisions as a single mother with two children. I also learned firsthand there is help for you but you will have to learn and to learn you must first be open to the idea of discipline.

Prayer Challenge

Pray for your acceptance of discipline.

Proverbs 12:1 "to learn, you must love discipline; it is stupid to hate correction."

_____

_____

_____

_____

_____

_____

_____

_____

_____

_____

_____

_____

_____

_____

_____

_____

_____

_____

_____

_____

_____

_____

_____

_____

Day 5

Today begin with your thank you prayer for being alive and having a life purpose that is dedicated to God's use.

"And we know that in all things God works for the good of those who love him, who have been called according to his purpose" (Romans 8:28).

One of the hardest things to do when you feel as if you have been victimized is to be wise in what you say. When your divorce is a result of an affair this is one of the areas that you see the tongue moving a lot. I personally found myself so upset after my second divorce that I contacted his family, friends, even his mistress. I was so hurt I had to make sure I would hurt him and humiliate him as he humiliated me. I wanted to seem as if I was better off without him and how terrible he was. Opening my mouth in such a way ruined many things for me. I was so angry and spiteful it spilled over into every other relationship I had and I didn't even realize it. Relationships I had as a mother, daughter, sister, aunt, friend, coworker, etc.... In thinking that I would feel better, I actually felt worse, obsessive, and I made it so uncomfortable for those around me. I spoke ruin over all areas and aspects of my

17

life. Please understand that the feeling of validation for trying to get back at the person who hurt you is temporary. It's the same as putting a band aid over a gash in your leg that needs stitches. You can keep band aids on it, however over time it will continue to bleed, become infected and you could lose that leg if not treated properly. Stop feeding the negativity in your life. It's not worth the pain you are causing yourself in the long run.

Prayer Challenge

Pray to God for discernment in the words you speak moving forward.

Proverbs 13:3 "Those who control their tongue will have a long life; opening your mouth can ruin everything."

_____

_____

_____

_____

_____

_____

_____

_____

_____

_____

_____

_____

_____

_____

_____

_____

_____

_____

_____

_____

_____

_____

Day 6

Today begin with your thank you prayer for being alive and having a life purpose that is dedicated to God's use.

"And we know that in all things God works for the good of those who love him, who have been called according to his purpose" (Romans 8:28).

The first few months after my 2nd divorce finalized I was upset. Yes I had friends who would ask what's wrong and I would be quick to share everything my ex did wrong. However, every time one hurt conversation led to another and another and once I looked back I wished I would have been more selective of what I said and who I said it to. For me I talked too much and filtered nothing. Sometimes I could feel myself just rambling however I felt the need that I needed to continue stating my case after the divorce finalized. This is not uncommon when you have encountered a divorce. Neither is it done purposely however, you have a sense of wanting to win the audience in your favor like an attorney giving their closing argument. Please know ladies that this only gives you temporary satisfaction. Looking back at the big picture I was stuck in my failed divorce by creating and securing the identity of the victim. I assumed the victim mentality and focused every breath I had on it unintentionally. I personally went to friends and continued to keep talking and growing my identity of a victim because I was safe there. Now in no way am I advocating to not speak to counselor, friend , or loved one when you feel you have hit rock bottom and you need help because you are having a hard time coping, or you just need a listening ear. This challenge is for someone who is stuck in telling their story every day to any and everyone who will listen. To the woman who (like me) in the past found a way to work the conversation of divorce into any topic that is mentioned. For example, someone asks how is the weather? Your response is the "weather feels just like the day my ex left me for another woman". Then that one question of how is the weather led to 2 hours of conversation about the new girlfriend/wife of your ex and your issues and concerns. This is unhealthy for you because you are not focused on your healing, you are focused on reopening the very wound that you are praying and asking God to heal. Continuing this conversation to point out how the others treated you or what you feel about them led you into a judgmental state of mind. The bible states in Matthew 7:1-2 do not judge others, and you will not be judged. For you will be treated as you treat others. The standard you use in judging is the standard by which you will be judged. I do not know about you ladies but I have not lived a perfect life therefore, I do not want to be judged by my past.

Prayer Challenge

Ask God to deliver you from the judgmental mindset that you currently have towards your ex and anyone associated with your ex.

Proverbs 10:19 "Too much talk leads to sin. Be sensible and keep your mouth shut."

_____

_____

_____

_____

_____

_____

_____

_____

_____

_____

_____

_____

_____

_____

_____

_____

_____

_____

_____

_____

_____

_____

Day 7

Today begin with your thank you prayer for being alive and having a life purpose that is dedicated to God's use.

"And we know that in all things God works for the good of those who love him, who have been called according to his purpose" (Romans 8:28).

My second marriage came upon the heels of my first divorce. When my first marriage ended I was devastated. We were young and listened to everyone and anyone's advice which ultimately led to the advice given to me to just get a divorce. I was even told before the ink was dry on the divorce decree, I needed to date and this led to a second marriage shortly after. Everyone around me told me that was what I needed to do. Yes, I can grieve but get over it be a victor, not a victim. I was told to get over the hurt and the pain and just move on. Some would also tell me the quicker I did this the faster I can heal. This sounded good to me seeing that the pain of my first divorce was so unbearable I was desperate for anything at that point. So as a result, I remarried and decided my goal in my second marriage was to make it as perfect as possible. Fix what I did wrong the first time so that this would never happen again. At least that was the lie that I believed. Get someone else, correct your mistakes, move on, and get over it. Well, unfortunately I did not realize that the enemy wanted me to believe that this was the way to heal from my divorce. This tactic was an effort to pull me further from the love of Christ by setting unrealistic expectations on myself. None of us are perfect and in believing that I was perfect or could obtain perfection was totally missing out on any spiritual growth that God had for me. In setting perfection in self or a relationship I was saying I myself do not need Jesus. If all is perfect what can Jesus do for me? Now I didn't walk around saying this out loud. No, I was the one that would tell anyone in a heartbeat Jesus Christ is my Lord and savior and I depend on Jesus for everything while my actions were totally opposite. When Jesus looked at my heart the words didn't matter my actions spoke louder. The enemy endorsed this with what appeared to me to be a life that I could achieve with a perfect marriage, job, and kids.

Prayer Challenge

Pray and ask God today to keep you authentic. If you're not having a good day, know that it's okay to lean on God to get you through. Do not try to fix your day by trying to create perfection yourself. Do not lean on your understanding in belief that you can achieve a perfect life.

Proverbs 3:5 "Trust in the LORD with all your heart and lean not on your own understanding"

_____

_____

_____

_____

_____

_____

_____

_____

_____

_____

_____

_____

_____

_____

_____

_____

_____

_____

_____

_____

_____

Day 8

Today begin with your thank you prayer for being alive and having a life purpose that is dedicated to God's use.

"And we know that in all things God works for the good of those who love him, who have been called according to his purpose" (Romans 8:28).

Many of us have encountered grief of some kind in our life prior to divorce. When I divorced both times it felt as if was grieving the death of a spouse but my spouse wasn't deceased. I remember the lie I believed at this point in my life was that my only way out was taking my life. Yes I was planning my suicide because I felt I had no purpose anymore. The only thing that did make sense was I'm not a good example to my two daughters, I'm a failure and I can't even tell you how I failed, so who can I help when I can't even help myself? I'm damaged goods and worst of all God must not love me anymore; God is punishing me for something and I have no idea what I did. Then it seemed as if people and time were just passing me by. Every waking moment I felt as if no one was there to console me not even to even say "I feel your pain". I believed the lie that if I wasn't here anymore it would all be over. I would have no more pain, no more issues, and it would all be done. Unfortunately when I believed this lie nothing rational made sense anymore. There is a deception tactic of the enemy that will make you feel there is only one destructive path to travel and that you are the only one who must travel that road alone. I know there are some of you out there who feel this way that all hope is gone. You may not have any family and your friends may have sided with your ex-spouse. Please know that you are not alone. It doesn't matter if you grew up in the church or if you are a skeptic or unbeliever. All you have to do is call on the name of Jesus. No person can meet your need as Jesus can. No person can talk to you or console you like Jesus. The enemy comes to kill, steal, and destroy. Before you make any decision call on the name of Jesus. Just call him.

Prayer Challenge

For this challenge call on the name of Jesus and no matter what you are going through ask Jesus to meet you where you are and help you.

Proverbs 18:10 "The name of the LORD is a strong tower; the righteous run to it and are safe."

_____

_____

_____

_____

_____

_____

_____

_____

_____

_____

_____

_____

_____

_____

_____

_____

_____

_____

_____

_____

_____

_____

Day 9

Today begin with your thank you prayer for being alive and having a life purpose that is dedicated to God's use.

"And we know that in all things God works for the good of those who love him, who have been called according to his purpose" (Romans 8:28)

I know there are those of you like myself who read the last challenge and said well I will try but there is no guarantee. Charis has no idea what was done to me and you are absolutely correct. I have no earthly idea what you did or did not encounter. I do not know who initiated the divorce, who cheated, who left, who was abused, who was drinking, gambling, addicted or who got the worst end of the stick because their spouse just left with no warning. However, I do know this, we are now past the divorce process and we are now into the life after divorce stage which is the recovery of your life. The definition of discretion as Webster's Dictionary describes it as "the quality of having or showing discernment or good judgment the quality of being discreet; especially cautious in speech". This rings so true at least in my actions regarding my divorce. I had both experiences myself because I left one marriage and in the next my ex-husband left me. I was so hurt in both situations that I spewed it out for all to hear. The only thing I accomplished was the fact that I was successful in becoming a gold ring in a pig's snout. Ladies please know that I do not know your situation and I do not need to know because God knows. There is no need to spread anger and hurt to others no matter how vindicated you believe it makes you feel. You can never obtain the vengeance that our God can obtain. Let go and Let God fight your battle.

Prayer Challenge

Pray for peace to let go and let God fight your battles.

Proverbs 11:22 "A beautiful woman who lacks discretion is like a gold ring in a pig's snout."

_____

_____

_____

_____

_____

_____

_____

_____

_____

_____

_____

_____

_____

_____

_____

_____

_____

_____

_____

_____

Day 10

Today begin with your thank you prayer for being alive and having a life purpose that is dedicated to God's use.

"And we know that in all things God works for the good of those who love him, who have been called according to his purpose" (Romans 8:28).

Sadly, for some regardless of how your divorce has ended thoughts of revenge, spitefulness, hurt, vengeance, etc... Will all come flooding in after your divorce at some time. I would like to devote this particular challenge to the woman who feels that she is a victim, just as I felt during and after my second divorce. The enemy can really wreak havoc in your life because you will feel justified in whatever you do. There is no boundary for you because boundaries resemble suffering and vulnerability. I want you to know no matter what you do vengeance in particular is not Godly. Please know that one day they will also be judged by our Heavenly father and so will you regarding your actions in the matter. Will you be able to stand and say confidently I did as you asked Father I loved those who hurt me? I did not seek vengeance nor validate it with justification. Or, will you stand before God saying I'm sorry I was wrong but it was justified God.

Prayer Challenge

Pray for boundaries, discernment, and understanding in your life.

Proverbs 11:23 "The godly can look forward to a reward, while the wicked can expect only judgment."

_____

_____

_____

_____

_____

_____

_____

_____

_____

_____

_____

_____

_____

_____

_____

_____

_____

_____

_____

_____

_____

Day 11

Today begin with your thank you prayer for being alive and having a life purpose that is dedicated to God's use.

"And we know that in all things God works for the good of those who love him, who have been called according to his purpose" (Romans 8:28).

It is so easy to not be truthful when you are hurt. I remember telling someone I'm good, this divorce is nothing to me I have been there done that. Unfortunately, that was far from the truth and ultimately it led to attempted suicide. I internalized all my hurt and pain because that is what a strong woman is supposed to do right? It's a sign of weakness in our society to ask for help or to show that we are human and we hurt. I actually have a name I created for this specific time in my life. I was no other than the "Great Pretender". Have you ever met the Great Pretender? Better yet are you living the life of The Great Pretender right now? Well just in case you are wondering who she is here are a few clues to see if you know her. The Great Pretender will smile daily and seem always to be positive; she encourages others, and even sets the bar as far as accomplishments and goals. She smiles and seems as if she has truly overcome her trials.

Occasionally she will get upset but very rarely and she always seems to get it back together. When you ask her how she does it she may say "only by the grace of God." Better yet she may tell you about her prayer life and also offer to even pray with you. But when she is around you feel something isn't right. She says the right things and she has it together but something still just isn't right. She has trained herself to be the Great Pretender. Not because she wants to lie no, it's just the opposite. Our society in many cases will tell those who are broken that there is no place for them. If you're broken you are weak and if you are weak you are not normal until you fix it. If you are broken in our society today you are looked down on as either in pity, charity, and at times alienated. You are told things such as oh it's just a divorce you will get over it, or we all have been through it just start a new relationship and move on. But then that day comes when you come to work and you hear the Great Pretender isn't ok, she has had a breakdown or just hit rock bottom, maybe even attempted suicide, or even worse she took her life. You pity her and don't understand why she is going through what she is going through. Why did she lie and what good did it do her? You learn later that she didn't sleep much or all she could do is sleep from her depression. She is sick to her stomach daily and when she looks in the mirror she sees the reflection of a stranger possibly even a monster as I did myself. She is lonely even when surrounded by a crowd of people who love her. Her relationships are not real and the life she created for you to see is really not her life. However what everyone fails to see is that she is pretending because she is in so much pain spiritually, emotionally and physically. She has trapped herself in a box to a point where she starts to panic because she can't breathe. She gives her all and helps everyone else and then the days begin to come when the enemy says to her "no one can help you."   However, there is help and it is through God. Now I can speak to this because when I was about to attempt suicide this is the box that I was in. I was in the box that I created and I felt at one time I could not find my way out. If you ever hit this point stop and call on the name of Jesus. It doesn't have to be a prayer, a song, or a rehearsed technique. When I was broken the last thing I could do was formulate a fancy prayer or even sing a song word for word. Just call on Jesus as I did over and over again. Scream or whisper either way call on the name Jesus. You will soon realize that with you in the quiet Jesus is and has always been there.

Prayer Challenge

Pray for deliverance of the Great Pretender mindset.
Instead ask God for a Godly mindset instead.

Proverbs 18:10 "The name of the LORD is a strong fortress; the godly run to him and are safe."

_____

_____

_____

_____

_____

_____

_____

_____

_____

_____

_____

_____

_____

_____

_____

_____

_____

_____

_____

_____

_____

_____

_____

_____

_____

_____

_____

_____

_____

_____

_____

_____

_____

_____

_____

_____

_____

_____

_____

_____

_____

_____

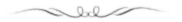

Day 12

Today begin with your thank you prayer for being alive and having a life purpose that is dedicated to God's use.

"And we know that in all things God works for the good of those who love him, who have been called according to his purpose" (Romans 8:28).

I remember hearing a lot of wise advice from people that I truly believe now looking back, God sent them across my path. However I despised hearing advice from others especially those who encountered a divorce. I would get angry when I would receive sound advice because I believed that the person giving the advice wanted only to draw attention to their so called testimony and remove all focus from me, my hurts, and my pain. The enemy was successful in convincing me to tune others out especially their testimony.   Now let me clarify this a little bit ladies. The attention that I wanted was toward my situation. This was not all the time but some of the time, I wanted this because I was comfortable being hurt during this particular time in my life. I taught myself to live in it, because I believed I deserved it. Restoration of any kind was impossible for me to imagine, let alone attempt to live it due to my two divorces which in my opinion was a punishment from God. I initiated a divorce from my first husband so when my second husband left that was my payback. I brainwashed myself to identify myself as a broken divorced woman with 2 kids, used goods, and not valuable to anyone. Now some of you may read this and say well you are a woman, you divorced, and you have two kids. However, it wasn't until I realized my true identity which is, I am the daughter of a king and my identity comes from HIM. Ladies guess what you are also the daughter of a King and your identity comes from HIM. It was then that I understood that I'm Charis the daughter of the Most High God, mother of two beautiful daughters, and yes I have encountered divorce.

Prayer Challenge

Whatever the reason for your divorce if you feel as if you are punishing yourself ask God for a release of all guilt you may be holding towards yourself.

Proverbs 13:13 "People who despise advice are asking for trouble; those who respect a command will succeed."

Day 13

Today begin with your thank you prayer for being alive and
having a life purpose that is dedicated to God's use.

*"And we know that in all things God works for the good of
those who love him, who have been called according to his
purpose" (Romans 8:28).*

Have you ever heard of someone who has made the
statement like "I wish I could have had this or that but it's
not going to happen for me? " In the early stages of
divorce I would look at married couples and their families
and say the same thing. Comments such as "must be nice"
or "she just doesn't realize how good she has it" were my
top two hopeless phrases. Yes I created hopeless phrases
to secure my sense of hopelessness. I would even speak
this in the presence of my kids with comments such as
"now you know we can't afford that" and "things are
different now we can't have that". So what was wrong
with this way of thinking? I personally removed hope from
my vocabulary and my life after my divorce. I let a tragic
event in my life (divorce) dictate if I and my girls should
have hope. Sounds crazy but a lot of us do it. It wasn't until
I started speaking hope in our lives I saw change. To be
honest I was just testing it to see if it would work and
guess what ladies? It did. I removed myself from my

negative associates. Yes negative must stay around negativity to feed itself. So long story short I lost many friends in my life. However, I made a decision to place myself around positive speaking people and it worked. When I went from saying "we won't be able to buy a house" to saying over and over again "I will buy a house", we actually bought a house. When I went from saying "I will never get a job working from home" to one day "I will work from home", I got the job working from home. Now I will say this it wasn't overnight please don't think that I bought a home over night or got a job the next day. Now it took time and in both of these cases a lot of time, but I never gave up on the hope that I would one day have the things I desire for me and my daughters.

Prayer Challenge

Ask God to remove the "I can't have the desires of my heart" mindset to the "If this is the desire of my heart and it's in God will I will have this and much more" mindset.

Proverbs 13:12 "Hope deferred makes the heart sick, but a dream fulfilled is a tree of life."

_____

_____

_____

_____

_____

_____

_____

_____

_____

_____

_____

_____

_____

_____

_____

_____

_____

_____

Day 14

Today begin with your thank you prayer for being alive and having a life purpose that is dedicated to God's use.

"And we know that in all things God works for the good of those who love him, who have been called according to his purpose" (Romans 8:28).

Have you ever watched a game show like Price is Right and the contestant is looking in the audience at whoever came with them to make the decision of spinning the wheel again? I ask myself why in the world would they spin the wheel again and the have 90 points, I mean really the odds of you getting 10 is slim to none and you are already ahead of the game. It doesn't seem that wise to me but hey to each his own, I would tell myself as the contestant strikes out and I turn the channel. Divorce I have learned causes us to spin the wheel again. Except there isn't anyone in the audience, we are spinning our wheels off of emotions such as anger, hurts, pains and much more. In my early days after divorce the voice of loneliness was calling my name. It was telling me "spin the wheel again come on you can do it." So how did I respond? You guessed it I started dating and serial dating at that, so I technically spun the wheel several times and associated myself with foolishness and not wisdom. Now my goal wasn't to be in a relationship with anyone. I just had this urge or sense I needed to feel wanted and the sense that someone wanted me. So with that in mind I wanted to pick up a phone and talk to a man, or call him up and go out when that feeling came. So let's talk a little about my feeling of loneliness. It took me awhile to realize that my feeling was a trigger or an alert for me to spend time with God. Loneliness was the ringing of my door bell to come spend time with God. However as we know we have a choice and instead of me answering the door I picked up the phone to search for someone to talk to. My wiring was weak (vulnerable) as if the doorbell was connected to the phone and this caused the electrical source to split and weaken. Its time ladies that we rewire ourselves to understand our needs will be provided from one source, which is God. If you do not take anything out of this challenge today please take this with you. Your loneliness can not be fulfilled by a person. I repeat YOUR LONELINESS CAN NOT BE FULFILLED BY ANY PERSON. Please set boundaries and do not associate with men on intimate levels out of loneliness after your divorce, let's be wise ladies. Otherwise you are becoming the game contestant that spins the wheel again when you have 90 points out of 100 and no one else is spinning behind you.

Prayer Challenge

Pray that your loneliness (void) is filled with God and God only.

Proverbs 13:20 "Walk with the wise and become wise; associate with fools and get in trouble."

_____
_____
_____
_____
_____
_____
_____
_____
_____
_____
_____
_____
_____
_____
_____
_____
_____
_____
_____
_____
_____
_____

Day 15

Today begin with your thank you prayer for being alive and having a life purpose that is dedicated to God's use.

"And we know that in all things God works for the good of those who love him, who have been called according to his purpose" (Romans 8:28).

Ladies you are created for fellowship and to have a relationship with God. When you starve that relationship (do not spend time with God in prayer, Bible study, confession, etc.) you trigger an alert (loneliness). We have been told by society that another person can erase loneliness especially when we are divorced. However please understand NO person can completely take your loneliness away. People will temporarily distract the void or mask the feeling, but understand loneliness will return if you do not respond to it appropriately. I had to learn the hard way however I have hope this will help you to see where I made one of my biggest mistakes. When you grasp this you will better understand the process of your individual healing and your decisions, directions, and choices will become wiser in your steps because you will understand your own personal blueprint to healing is thru God and God's word.

Prayer Challenge

Pray for your relationship with Jesus and that daily it strengthens as you encounter your healing.

Proverbs 14:15 "Only simpletons believe everything they're told! The prudent carefully consider their steps."

61

_____

_____

_____

_____

_____

_____

_____

_____

_____

_____

_____

_____

_____

_____

_____

_____

_____

_____

_____

_____

_____

_____

Day 16

Today begin with your thank you prayer for being alive and having a life purpose that is dedicated to God's use.

"And we know that in all things God works for the good of those who love him, who have been called according to his purpose" (Romans 8:28).

Would you ever build a home with your bare hands just to tear it all down when you discover a few bricks were broken in transit? Yes the bricks were special ordered and even though they are not absolutely impossible to get back you know the probability for you to get them replaced may be slim to none. Some will tell you just go and get some other bricks however the danger in that is those bricks are being picked out of desperation. They may seem easy to obtain and you can finish building the house, however at the first sight of rain you find out these bricks do not fit at all. You are dealing with flooding, water damage, and even a bigger mess at times to begin with. So what do we do in this case? Well normally we call in an expert one who can assess the damage and give a suggestion of an alternative for us. Many times we get upset because of the time or the cost but at the end we know the finished work will be beautiful so we pay the price and we wait. So I'm curious why will we allow an expert contractor to come in and repair our home and be patient with that and not do the same with our own personal expert Jesus Christ. Why not allow Jesus to come in and repair us. Let's be wise ladies and build our homes wisely in order to not be so hasty and tear them down with our own hands.

Prayer Challenge

Pray for your acceptance of your healing through Jesus Christ

Proverbs 14:1 "A wise woman builds her home, but a foolish woman tears it down with her own hands."

_____
_____
_____
_____
_____
_____
_____
_____
_____
_____
_____
_____
_____
_____
_____
_____
_____
_____
_____
_____
_____
_____
_____
_____

Day 17

Today begin with your thank you prayer for being alive and having a life purpose that is dedicated to God's use.

"And we know that in all things God works for the good of those who love him, who have been called according to his purpose" (Romans 8:28).

My kids would make comments when they thought I didn't hear them talking once they were in bed. Whenever I had a really bad day, which seemed to be daily at one point in time, they would make jokes that mommy is in her dark space. It was funny to me at first to think that the kids would say that and I thought it was kind of cute because kids will say the craziest things. Until one night I heard my youngest ask my oldest "why is mom always in her dark space"? And my oldest responded with "it's the new mom they do that after a divorce because she is unhappy". My youngest followed that comment with "Oh so she will never be happy again. I just want her happy again I want our mom back". To hear this was such a painful experience as a parent however for those who do not have children what about our friends and loved ones who feel this way. There is going to be a period of where you will go through as my kids described in their words "dark space" which translates to unhappiness and brokenness. Face it no matter how your divorce ends you may be unhappy about the number of years you went through, or your change of financial status, relocating and starting over, parenting plans, increased work hour, less time with kids, etc. So unhappiness isn't just stemming from the relationship it can come from several other aspects also. I have heard women mention that they are not upset about the divorce anymore but it is now more so an inconvenience for them. Whatever the case may be for you relational or inconvenience my point is please try not to get stuck in it no matter your reason. Years of unhappiness daily are is dangerous and you do not need to suffer through this alone. There are coaches and counselors out there for you and you don't have to walk this walk alone. Please do not do as I did and wait 3 years please seek help as soon as you are able to. Many local churches offer free counseling sessions and yearly seminars. Some churches do not require membership for you to attend. You can also check out our events on The Divorce Recovery Advocates Working for Women website which is www.draw4women.com. Whatever you do I ask that you please stop and invest time in yourself because if you do not invest in yourself you cannot fully invest in others.

Prayer Challenge

Pray to invest into yourself and not feel guilty for doing so.

Proverbs 14:10 "Each heart knows its own bitterness, and no one else can fully share its joy."

_____

_____

_____

_____

_____

_____

_____

_____

_____

_____

_____

_____

_____

_____

_____

_____

_____

_____

_____

_____

_____

_____

Day 18

Today begin with your thank you prayer for being alive and having a life purpose that is dedicated to God's use

"And we know that in all things God works for the good of those who love him, who have been called according to his purpose" (Romans 8:28).

When I divorced I noticed a big shift in my life. It seemed to come in the area of friends. I lost a lot of friends and I was so confused about this because the majority of these friends were not even friends of my ex-husbands. I mean I have heard many people speak on if you have mutual friends they will pick sides, so in a sense I was prepared for that. What I wasn't prepared for was my friends jumping ship. This was really difficult for me and I noticed a pattern. It seemed to mostly be my married friends. I no longer had a place in the group and I became the outsider. This was very hurtful because I was the same person who organized the group. I now can see looking back that truth will show up and will clean up in every area of your life once you ask God to reveal truth through your prayers. I say this because my divorce showed me, who was really there for me and, who was there when it was convenient to be there for me. Then on the other hand there were my single friends who were there to just update me on the drama. Specifically drama at times that I didn't even know I had. As a women who has went through two divorces you need true authentic relationships with friends who are there to help and encourage you and not try to dig and process what happened in the past or encourage spitefulness, unforgiveness, or vengeance. A friend doesn't come and tell you everything your ex is up to right now with his new spouse or new life. Please understand that is not blessing you in any way and you need to inform that person that you are divorced, rebuilding your life, and you prefer to no longer be updated on your ex's life. Once again please do not fall into the trap of getting constant updates on the progress of your ex-husband. This will severely slow down your own personal healing process and in some cases stop it completely.

Prayer Challenge

Pray for the authentic Godly relationships in your life rather they are old or brand new.

Proverbs 14:20 "The poor are despised even by their neighbors, while the rich have many friends."

_____

_____

_____

_____

_____

_____

_____

_____

_____

_____

_____

_____

_____

_____

_____

_____

_____

_____

_____

_____

_____

_____

_____

Day 19

Today begin with your thank you prayer for being alive and having a life purpose that is dedicated to God's use.

"And we know that in all things God works for the good of those who love him, who have been called according to his purpose" (Romans 8:28).

For me personally I remembered struggling in many areas of my life after my divorce such as financial, emotional, spiritual, parenting, social, and many more areas I could list. Heck to be honest if it was an area of my life I had issues with it. However parenting seemed to be one of a few that I could not place on hold to allow myself time to recover. I had to face it. Kids cannot wait on their needs to allow time for their parent to grieve. For example, you may not want to eat but guess what you still will need to get up out the bed and feed your children daily. I remember one day I dragged myself to the kitchen to cook for the kids and I was determined to strategize my life back into order before my biscuits came out. I sat at the table waiting on biscuits in the oven and bullet pointed my life but I discovered there were several different paths I could take. I spent relentless hours trying to decide if I should move or should I stay, should I change jobs or should I get a second job, better yet should I keep the kids in the same school and commute to work or relocate and change everything. Like I said I was seriously bullet pointing my life. Unknowingly I was trying to construct my life outline without my one true source which is God who is the author of my story. I would suggest that you do not try to write the final draft of your life just as I tried. To be honest Gods story is much better than you could ever imagine for yourself. I would like to challenge you to place your trust in God today and allow God to enter your life and write your story. For one day do not plan anything and I mean absolutely anything. It's ok if you cannot do it today but try to do this before your 30 day challenge is completed. You will be amazed at where God will take you and your children or loved ones in your life if you just let HIM guide you.

Prayer Challenge

Ask God to lead you today not just for yourself but for your children and loved ones.

Proverbs 3:6 "seek his will in all you do, and he will show you which path to take."

_____

_____

_____

_____

_____

_____

_____

_____

_____

_____

_____

_____

_____

_____

_____

_____

_____

_____

_____

_____

_____

Day 20

Today begin with your thank you prayer for being alive and having a life purpose that is dedicated to God's use.

"And we know that in all things God works for the good of those who love him, who have been called according to his purpose" (Romans 8:28).

In the beginning right after my divorce I had a terrible temper. Some days I didn't even want to have a bad temper but it was more natural for me to have a hot temper than to have a cool one. Especially when my ex would call regarding our kids, I would make sure that day that someone got a piece of the hot temper. It came to the point where no one wanted to deal with me. One day I realized that wasn't me and the divorce was over. It was time to stop holding the anger within myself and boiling over every time I went somewhere or spoke to someone. I was tired of looking for confrontation and ways to be loud and argue. This wasn't effective for me and neither was it for my kids and loved ones. So I started to operate in the mentality that peace was more important to me than war. When I started to embrace peace I noticed things that once were not in my favor would now change to be in my favor. I was blessed when my temper was calm.

Prayer Challenge

Pray for deliverance from a hot temper.

Proverb 15:18 "A hot-tempered person starts fights; a cool-tempered person stops them."

_____

_____

_____

_____

_____

_____

_____

_____

_____

_____

_____

_____

_____

_____

_____

_____

_____

_____

_____

_____

_____

_____

Day 21

Today begin with your thank you prayer for being alive and having a life purpose that is dedicated to God's use.

"And we know that in all things God works for the good of those who love him, who have been called according to his purpose" (Romans 8:28).

Pride and arrogance were embedded in my thoughts after my second marriage. I was so determined to not really tell anyone how much I was suffering out of pride. I also had this attitude because I had divorced before and I didn't feel I needed anyone to help me. When I was hurt I felt as if I couldn't show it. Reality was I had taken two huge financial blows in a course of a few short years. If I needed something definitely this was the time that I needed it. I remember as a single mom one day our company had a huge catered potluck. At the end of the potluck a member of our planning committee made the comment saying "I know this could probably help you would you like to take these left overs for you and the kids". Now reality was yes this meal would have blessed us however pride and arrogance caused me to say no and then the fall came as I stood there and watched food go into the trash that had never been opened. There were selections of sandwiches wrapped perfectly with juices, fruits, drinks, and cookies. All of it would have definitely lasted us a couple days until my next payday. I thought it was the worst thing that I could ever have seen until I got home and my kids were hungry. That was truly the fall when I realized I passed up a blessing out of my own selfishness that impacted my kids. I know there are some ladies out there just like I was so prideful and arrogant out of pain and brokenness. Understand that you aren't taking a hand out; you are taking a blessing that God has provided for you through sources you may not have imagined. While you are busy worrying about how to stretch $5 towards gas and food, you have been given food that will supply your need until your next paycheck. If you are not working then this blessing will carry you to the next one. Never be ashamed to feed yourself or your children as I was. Speak up and remember that pride and arrogance will cause destruction in your life.

Prayer Challenge

Pray for the release of the prideful spirit that you are carrying.

Proverbs 16:18 "Pride goes before destruction and haughtiness before a fall."

_____

_____

_____

_____

_____

_____

_____

_____

_____

_____

_____

_____

_____

_____

_____

_____

_____

_____

_____

_____

_____

_____

_____

Day 22

Today begin with your thank you prayer for being alive and having a life purpose that is dedicated to God's use.

"And we know that in all things God works for the good of those who love him, who have been called according to his purpose" (Romans 8:28).

Closest friends and family definitely gave me their opinions once they discovered I was getting a divorce. I was told by many to hurry up and date someone else. Well needless to say I tried it because at the time it sounded like a great idea. But as we all know those great ideas do not always turn out to be what God has planned ahead in life for you. I had to take a step back and learn this lesson on my own. Let's just say this one was my trial, error, crash, and burn lesson. In life you more than likely already know its ok if you try some advice and if it doesn't work out; it's not the end of the world. In business this is called risk and I was taught in business school that your failed risks are learning opportunities for what to do or not to do next time. You may or may not encounter them but if you do they will actually teach you how to be successful in the future. Think of this challenge with the strategic mindset of how you respond to your divorce and how you can prepare yourself in case a challenging situation arises in the near future. When a business decision has encountered a risk and it has failed the owner is not deemed a failure in life, so why do we feel we are a failure after divorce? When you encounter a divorce it's easy to sometimes want to go back and fix your past by replacing your ex with a new and improved mate just to see if you can change the outcome now to be in your favor. That feeling of failure and I have to fix this, will creep up on you and I will be the first to tell you that that is a deception the enemy has told many of us. The truth is you can't go back to the past hour or past five minutes let along go back to the past to fix what could have been. Ladies we must focus on the present and not the past. Stop looking back into what once was happy or even sad days to try to rewrite them. When you do this you are cheating yourself from progressing through your healing stages and also you cheat yourself from looking forward into your joyful days. Yes you can look at memories but know that they are just those; memories. Do not dwell on memories of the past when you can be living in the present moments and discovering what God has already orchestrated for you today.

Prayer Challenge

Today ask God for direction in your life and also peace in knowing that God will direct you and you are not a failure.

Proverbs 4:25 "Look straight ahead, and fix your eyes on what lies before you."

_____

_____

_____

_____

_____

_____

_____

_____

_____

_____

_____

_____

_____

_____

_____

_____

_____

_____

_____

_____

Day 23

Today begin with your thank you prayer for being alive and having a life purpose that is dedicated to God's use.

"And we know that in all things God works for the good of those who love him, who have been called according to his purpose" (Romans 8:28).

Another area that was hard for me right after my divorce was the fact that I actually thought that I knew it all after having the second divorce. I started to take on a role of being an expert for women who had recently divorced. During this time I was living dangerously because I felt I had no need to pray or involve God or Jesus because I got this, I lived it, and why should I pray about it. Funny thing is it wasn't working and I learned really quickly I was in denial. I couldn't succeed at my two marriages so I told myself I must succeed in helping others in order to heal myself. In other words I could tell others how to cope with life after divorce but I could not cope with the process of applying my own advice for myself. I actually had a plan, it was to go to every workshop possible on divorce, go to some bible study classes, and buy some books from several Bookstores to start a library collection on the topic of divorce. Then I had plans to pour all of this expertise back into other women. Problem with this way of thinking was I placed my trust in all of these tasks and not in God and this is because I didn't allow Jesus to heal me in the first place. I would like to give you the best advice I have ever received and applied in my life from a friend of mine. One day we were sitting and I was complaining about all the tasks I had and she said "Charis why don't you try to seek Jesus for your healing and no other people, tasks, objects, or even yourself".

Prayer Challenge

Pray for understanding of God will for your journey in life.

Proverbs 12:15 "Fools think their own way is right, but the wise listens to others".

_____
_____
_____
_____
_____
_____
_____
_____
_____
_____
_____
_____
_____
_____
_____
_____
_____
_____
_____
_____
_____
_____

Day 24

Today begin with your thank you prayer for being alive and having a life purpose that is dedicated to God's use.

"And we know that in all things God works for the good of those who love him, who have been called according to his purpose" (Romans 8:28).

I remember seeing a friend post beautiful pictures of what looked to be an awesome vacation she took on Facebook. When I called to get details she said to me "Charis it was the worst vacation ever. They lost my luggage, my room was not ready, and I ate something I was allergic to". After we laughed about it I got off the phone and thought wow looking at this awesome picture is such an illusion. Then I looked at myself and said wow my life was just that an illusion. On the outside I looked like a great woman who has overcome not one but two divorces and is working and successfully getting back up on her feet. However that wasn't the case at all that was my illusion that I created for all to see. This is also where the enemy came in and stole my joy from within. My ability to hide my pain grew stronger day by day. Just as my joy and healing were draining right out of my life. The lie grew bigger and I grew more distant. I remember feeling so out of place one day when a friend of mine said "Charis I don't know how you can do it you are a strong woman". Yes in a sense I felt like I finally made it and I was that strong woman who needed no one. I had overcome with my own strength and was progressing forward on my own. Everything on the outside was looking great. Single mother of two who lost everything now has a new home, new car, great job, enrolled back in college, making straight A's, and yes we are even taking family vacations now. So tell me why with all of these perfect things going on in my life why was I feeling like the vacation my friend took. It was the worst I had ever felt in my life but I appeared to be back on track and even better than ever. The best way I can describe it was like I was trapped in a sound proof box screaming but no one could hear me. See I tried to plan my course however my plans were not ordered by God. So my plan had a weak foundation. With this prayer challenge I would like to ask that you focus more on God's desire and purpose for you and not your own. How can you do this you may ask? You take this request to God through prayer.

Prayer Challenge

Pray to God for your purpose and passions to be revealed to you.

Proverbs 16:9 "In their hearts human beings plan their course, but the LORD establishes their steps."

_____

_____

_____

_____

_____

_____

_____

_____

_____

_____

_____

_____

_____

_____

_____

_____

_____

_____

_____

_____

_____

Day 25

Today begin with your thank you prayer for being alive and having a life purpose that is dedicated to God's use.

"And we know that in all things God works for the good of those who love him, who have been called according to his purpose" (Romans 8:28).

I have divorced twice and in that I have had two totally different experiences. After my first divorce I remember going into my boss's office with my supervisor and a couple other staff members to ask for a few days to recoup. In that meeting I was informed that what I shared in that room would stay in that room, so I opened completely up and told everything and I mean every little detail. Well a couple days later when I returned I was bombarded with questions of what happened, am I ok, awkward stares, glances that resembled a look of pity, and of course gossip. I remember that day wishing that there was another way I could have gone to my supervisors unidentified to ask for time off to recoup. I was now humiliated and my trust now for those in that room at my job was broken along with my life that was already feeling broken. Can you imagine going through a divorce and now having such a humiliating feeling that you decide to leave your job? Well, that happened to me, I had to leave because that feeling sickened me daily. I was so powerless over my life that I had to have a pity party thrown by people every day, who really didn't know me outside of work. Don't get me started on gossip; it was so out of hand I became severely depressed. The best way I can describe how I felt after these two life changing events was like two unstable molecules ready to react at a moment's notice. My advice to you is to use wisdom and discernment in what you share, especially with those who are not close to you. Your job is your professional workplace and the best advice I can give you is this: If you are uncomfortable with a stranger at work, do not do as I did and share intimate details about your divorce. Furthermore, do not sit with multiple people to share these details at work. Do not underestimate the destructive havoc that gossip can impose on your life in the workplace setting.

Prayer Challenge

Pray to God for discernment with which you should share what you are going through with your divorce.

Proverbs 11:13 "A gossip goes around telling secrets, but those who are trustworthy can keep a confidence."

Day 26

Today begin with your thank you prayer for being alive and having a life purpose that is dedicated to God's use.

"And we know that in all things God works for the good of those who love him, who have been called according to his purpose" (Romans 8:28).

I must say hatred and unforgiveness are two forces that no one should ever reckon with. Now of course I had to learn this the hard way. As I told you before I'm very hard headed.   Funny I thought I understood this the day my second husband contacted me to tell me he was sorry for his actions. I accepted and told him I had forgiven him however, I was really confused. I was still angry, upset, unhappy, and I had no idea why. Well the reason I didn't know why was because I never forgave myself. C. S Lewis said it best "To be a Christian means to forgive the inexcusable, because God has forgiven the inexcusable in you". So I forgave him but not myself now what?

I have come to learn it's not easy to forgive yourself in life. For me I didn't even understand why I was still stuck after the apology my ex-husband gave me. I started to build such a hatred and unforgiveness in my heart for myself. So where was all of this coming from? I decided to ignore it just as if you ignore an infection however, after some point that infection will become toxic and eat away at you. Underneath everything my unforgiveness and hatred was what I felt for myself. I couldn't believe how easy it was to forgive someone else who hurt me terribly and how difficult it was to forgive myself. From that day forward I became toxic because I shut down the ability to let love operate freely in my life. I now know and understand God is love and when I shut out love I shut out God in my life. It was not the circumstance of the divorce itself it was my reaction to the circumstance of the divorces and as a result I shut out my personal relationship with God. It was then that I understood I could not forgive myself because I was shutting God out of my life.

Prayer Challenge

Pray and ask God to help give you the strength that you
need to forgive no only those whom have hurt you but
also forgiveness for yourself

Proverbs 4:7 "Wisdom is supreme; therefore get wisdom.
Though it cost all you have, get understanding."

Day 27

Today begin with your thank you prayer for being alive and having a life purpose that is dedicated to God's use.

"And we know that in all things God works for the good of those who love him, who have been called according to his purpose" (Romans 8:28).

It's a process to your healing just as it is a process to learn how to go from crawling as a baby to walking as a toddler. If you have any unforgiveness in your heart please ask and allow Jesus Christ to come into your heart and mend it. Unforgiveness doesn't disappear on its own overnight. Forgiveness when truly experienced is a blessing beyond belief. When you forgive you are able to release yourself from being stuck in your past. If you stay in the past you will not see all the blessings that God has for you in the present. Your relationship with God is the key to success when it comes to forgiveness. Strengthening your relationship with God will bring understanding when it comes to forgiveness.

Prayer Challenge

Pray and ask for clarity on your relationship with God. Really pray today on ways to strengthen your relationship whether it is more time in God's word or even going and getting a bible so you can start reading Gods word.

Proverbs 4:5 "Get wisdom, get understanding; do not forget my words or turn away from them."

_____

_____

_____

_____

_____

_____

_____

_____

_____

_____

_____

_____

_____

_____

_____

_____

_____

_____

_____

_____

_____

_____

_____

_____

_____

_____

_____

_____

_____

_____

_____

_____

_____

_____

_____

_____

_____

_____

_____

_____

_____

_____

_____

_____

Day 28

Today begin with your thank you prayer for being alive and having a life purpose that is dedicated to God's use.

"And we know that in all things God works for the good of those who love him, who have been called according to his purpose" (Romans 8:28)

Have you ever heard the comment "Divorce brings the worst out of a person"? Well let's just say this is all too real for me. For myself there was a point where I was so hurt I used social media to vent my hurt against my ex-husband. This was what I thought would avenge my pain. I told myself that my cruelty would be momentarily validated. Afterwards it actually felt not valid at all; it was just hurtful and selfish acts on my part to hurt the people who I felt hurt me. It felt good after the act but slowly and surely I felt worse daily. I then began to spiral out of control into deeper depression and shortly after I attempted to commit suicide. I lived this personally and never ever in my life do I want anyone to choose cruelty, anger, hatred, or revenge. Through this the enemy will try to steal, kill, and destroy your life. These acts are like drinking toxic poison and waiting to see what it does to your ex. The poison is in your body and flowing through your veins. It is actually eating away at your organs and stopping your heart, not your ex-husband's. So let me ask a small favor instead of a challenge as I have done in the previous days. If you are being cruel towards anyone, whether it is due to their actions of what they have done to you or to ones you love, please stop. You are not destroying them, you are destroying yourself. Do not assassinate yourself to seek a false sense of healing. Your healing can be found in God alone. Place your trust in knowing this truth, God hurts when someone hurts you. Please allow God to handle that battle. "The Battle is not yours, it's the Lords." (2Chronicles 20:15)

Prayer Challenge

Pray to God to remove any cruelty you have in your heart and show you how to live again with kindness.

Proverbs 11:17 "Your kindness will reward you, but your cruelty will destroy you."

_____

_____

_____

_____

_____

_____

_____

_____

_____

_____

_____

_____

_____

_____

_____

_____

_____

_____

_____

_____

Day 29

Today begin with your thank you prayer for being alive and having a life purpose that is dedicated to God's use.

"And we know that in all things God works for the good of those who love him, who have been called according to his purpose" (Romans 8:28).

After my divorce my self-esteem was under attack. It's funny how you can get kicked once you're already down and not even know what happened to you. I was hurt by the decision my second husband made however what I was doing to myself as a result of his decision was where I went wrong. I remember looking in a mirror after I lost some weight physically thinking to myself that I looked healthier but I was looking at a stranger. The woman in that mirror was not Charis she looked familiar but she wasn't Charis. The reflection in the mirror wasn't who God created me to be. If I couldn't look in mirror and identify myself then who could? It took me some time to realize God created me uniquely just as he created everyone with their own uniqueness. As a child my mother would always say you are a "Divine Original". Believe it or not it actually took a flower telling me this for me to resurface what my mother told me and finally get it. Yes a flower a matter a fact the pseudanthium of a Sunflower. One day my old boss brought in a sunflower to work from her garden and placed it in a vase. That day I was so amazed at the beauty of the sunflower. God had actually taken the center of this flower and painted little yellow stars on her. Now if God took the time to paint stars on the sunflower then what did God draw within my heart I asked myself? I began to think it would be absolutely silly to me if this same sunflower thought she was not as beautiful because the other flowers around her were pulled from the ground. Would that circumstance in the garden change how God created her and her beauty? This is where I learned from the sunflower the beauty of what lies within us not within our circumstances.

Prayer Challenge

Today pray that God shows you your beauty. The only way that you will ever know your beauty is to be able to see it yourself.

Proverbs 8:22 "The LORD brought me forth as the first of his works, before his deeds of old;"

_____

_____

_____

_____

_____

_____

_____

_____

_____

_____

_____

_____

_____

_____

_____

_____

_____

_____

_____

_____

Day 30

Today begin with your thank you prayer for being alive and having a life purpose that is dedicated to God's use.

"And we know that in all things God works for the good of those who love him, who have been called according to his purpose" (Romans 8:28).

I know it's hard right now. I won't ask you to list what is hurting you the most because honestly you may not know or you may have too many to list. I too had this same issue. In my mind, I went into protect myself mode. Protecting myself means becoming someone that I'm not, a harsh cold woman who disliked mostly every sign of happiness that I saw. I believed this was an act of guarding my heart from ever being hurt again, so I validated this by saying to myself "I have to do what I have to do I'm in survival mood now." The truth is I wasn't guarding my heart at all. I was letting the very thing into my heart that I called myself keeping out." Ladies we must protect ourselves, but also know that protecting our heart is not hardening our hearts to those around us. The best example would be if you were feeding a child who seemed to not finish their food would you decrease the amount of food you're placing on their plate or would you not feed them at all? This is also true with your heart you can protect your heart by making necessary adjustments but also at the same time if you're not careful you can starve your heart.

Prayer Challenge

Ask God to continue to lead you in guarding your heart. Do not allow your divorce to cause you to guard your heart incorrectly. The feeling of hurt is not a reason to allow wrong things to flow from your heart.

Proverbs 4:23 "Above all else, guard your heart, for everything you do flows from it."

_____

_____

_____

_____

_____

_____

_____

_____

_____

_____

_____

_____

_____

_____

_____

_____

_____

_____

_____

_____

"O Lord, you have examined my heart and know everything about me. You know when I sit down and stand up. You know my thoughts even when I'm far away. You see me when I travel and when I rest at home. You know everything I do. You know what I am going to say even before I say it, Lord. You go before me and follow me. You place your hand of blessing on my head. Such knowledge is too wonderful for me, too great for me to understand! I can never escape from your Spirit! I can never get away from your presence! If I go up to heaven, you are there; if I go down to the grave, you are there If I ride the wings of the morning, if I dwell by the farthest oceans, even there your hand will guide me, and your strength will support me" Psalm 139 vs. 1-10

_____

_____

_____

_____

_____

_____

_____

_____

_____

_____

_____

_____

_____

_____

_____

_____

_____

_____

_____

_____

_____

_____

Meet the Author:
Charis Rooks

Divorce is not as cut and dried as everyone imagines it to be. It is a struggle, a challenge, and a true test of character. As not only a survivor but someone that flourished after divorce, Charis Rooks is ready to help inspire women going through the same struggle to rise up. Charis was able to move past her divorce to found Divorce Recovery Advocates Working for Women LLC (Draw for Women) a life after divorce recovery organization that focuses on forward movement and recovery for women after divorce.

As a woman who has been through divorce, Charis knows what it takes to become a strong independent woman despite the scars which divorce leaves. When she is not working to empower her fellow women, Charis loves spending time with her husband and together they strive to raise their daughters to become the strong women they both know they are destined to be. She and her family currently live in Kentucky where she has completed her Bachelor's degree in Business Technical Management with a concentration in Small Business Management and Entrepreneurship. Charis is currently pursuing her MBA in Leadership at Oral Roberts University. Charis leads by example and works to show women that though divorce can hurt a woman, it cannot break her.

Charis is passionate about speaking the truth and working to spread the word of Christ and its healing power. In addition to Draw for Women, Charis has also: been a speaker, a Life after Divorce Care facilitator and a facilitator for Divorce Care support groups. She is a Celebrate Recovery Training Coach, member of the Professional Women's Network, has taken part in the American Association of Christian Counselors, and the International Christian Coaching Association. Charis has also achieved several certifications including being certified as an International Women's Leadership Coach with a specialization in women's empowerment, confidence building and professionalism. She has also achieved certification with the American Association of Christian Counselors as a life coach with a specialization in life after divorce coaching. Charis is also the author of Gods Rarest Diamonds: A Proverbs life After Divorce Devotional for Women.

Charis is dedicated to her craft and to making sure that every woman who is struggling with divorce knows that there is hope, there is a way to succeed. Charis is a dedicated individual who wants nothing more than to share her ideas, experiences and knowledge to help other women who are struggling with divorce to become comfortable with themselves and with the state of their lives again.

Contact:
Charis Rooks
Divorce Recovery Advocates Working for Women LLC
http://www.draw4women.com
Email: info@draw4women.com
Facebook: http://facebook.com/draw4women
Facebook:
http://facebook.com/charismrooksoutreachministries
Twitter: Charis Rooks @draw4women
Instagram: Draw4Women

CPSIA information can be obtained
at www.ICGtesting.com
Printed in the USA
FFOW03n1218250217
32785FF